STRANGE,

UFO's & Aliens In My Life

By

E. A. Sabean

CHAPTER ONE

Life is full of irony and one of the most ironic things in my life is that I didn't always believe in UFO's or aliens from other worlds.

When I was a kid I was interested in UFO's and aliens but more from a science fiction standpoint. I mean, I also loved the Six Million Dollar Man but I knew he wasn't *real*.

When I was a teenager, I still had the interest in UFO's and aliens, but again, it was not a passion or anything. My science fiction type of interest in them had moved to more of a curiosity, wondering if the people that claimed to have seen such things were crazy or just made it all up. Either way, I did not think things like that really happened! I couldn't figure out for the life of me why people would make up such strange things and actually expect other people to believe it!

Sometime in the 80's I think, I cannot remember exactly when, a program came on TV about a guy named Jesse that was with the US Military at the time of the Roswell crash. This was the first I'd ever heard about Roswell. As I said, my previous interest in aliens and spaceships was more in the science fiction realm and involved things such as Escape To Witch Mountain and Star Trek, Battlestar Galactica, Lost In Space, etc.

Watching this old man on television explain details about the Roswell crash and cover up made me see UFO's in a whole new light.   This created a constant wavering between near belief and nonbelief for me. This Jesse guy seemed serious and honest and had pictures to prove it. While I was watching him speak, I believed him but as time passed my belief wavered and then disappeared.

Sure, I'd had unexplainable experiences in my life ever since I was a small child but they did not involve alien abduction, of that I was sure. Especially since I didn't believe it was possible.

However, my interest in the subject of UFO's grew and I read as many books as I could get my hands on, which only increased my wavering between belief and nonbelief in the subject.

There weren't that many TV shows on about people being abducted (at least that I saw), and even when I'd watch people tell with tears and convictions of their ordeals I did not believe they were being abducted by aliens from other planets! I did believe they believed they experienced *something* and maybe really did experience something, but it could not be aliens from other planets.

My conclusion about all of those things was that if anything was abducting people and doing any kind of genetic experiments on them, it *must* be the government doing it! Surely if the government were doing any such thing to people it would be in their best interest to either erase the victim's memory of the event or hypnotize them with a screen memory. This made sense to me. If the government had the inclination, skills and tools to perform genetic experiments, they most certainly had what it would take to make the victim not remember anything.

So, that became my final conclusion on the whole UFO and alien abduction thing. For the people that were not making up stories and telling outright lies, they obviously had been some part of government genetic or other type of experiment. Crashed saucers? Obviously failed experiments by our own Earthly governments!

My view on this caused many arguments with others that insisted 'our governments' would not do such things to their citizens. However, I felt firm to my conclusion on the matter since it was the only one that seemed sensible, real or even possible.

My conclusion about this was shattered when I had my first-that-I-recall adult encounter with small creatures that had entered my bedroom in the night, apparently coming in through the walls. These creatures that had invaded my bedroom, and my life, were not anything of this Earth. They were not human and they were not animals. They were not, I think, even of this dimension but they were very real. The technology or methods they used were not of this dimension, or at the very least, of anything currently available to the human race.

Once I had what I thought was my first encounter, since anything previously I had been convinced by my parents was a dream, my tune changed dramatically on what other people were claiming to have experienced.

Where I had not believed people before when they talked of seeing UFO's or aliens, I now believed them. I, myself, had seen beings that were not of this world. They had done things to me that were not humanly possible. They moved in ways that we did not move.

Even still, I did not believe these were aliens from other planets, but I no longer believed it was any kind of human government abducting people. I now believed that there were nonhuman forces behind these cases now. As far as the 'flying saucers' and strange lights in the skies, I hadn't seen any but obviously people were mistaking airplanes or clouds for UFO's. And lights? I mean, they were obviously seeing the International Space Station, Venus, Jupiter or some other natural source of light.

My views on the lights that other people claimed they saw changed as well once I saw lights myself. I've explained these in detail in a later chapter and have included sketches and drawings of the beings I've seen, and the lights in the sky I've seen.

Once I had my first visit from these creatures in my adult life (again, not counting the one that I had been convinced was a dream when I was a small child), I wanted desperately to find someone that had seen the same beings. I was disappointed to find that every description of alien being by other people looked absolutely nothing like the creatures I'd seen. Everyone seemed to see tall gray beings with spindly arms and slanted eyes. I'd seen tiny brown beings with monk-like hooded robes! The beings I'd seen had huge round eyes, not slanted.

It never occurred to me to write a book about the beings I'd seen. After all, my life was pretty uneventful, I thought. I saw strange creatures once and that was certainly not enough of an experience to fill a book! However, after having them visit me again ten years later, I began analyzing all the strange experiences in my life that started when I was a child. Things that were abnormal in my opinion and that made no sense to me and had always left me scrambling for explanations.

When it got to the point where I experienced for the first time (that I'm aware of) the phenomena of 'missing time', I began to think that there was more happening to me than I'd ever been aware of. As I pieced everything together and added up all the strangeness, I was alarmed to find that many of the details in the claims of those who said they had been abducted (that I had failed to believe), had actually been taking place in my own life . . . all the while I wasn't believing any such thing was even possible!

When this dawned on me, beginning with the realization that two and a half hours were missing from my morning, causing me to be late with my morning news deadlines and failing to record half of a talk show I was responsible for monitoring, I felt I had to write a book. I had to speak out about the strange things that had happened in my life. I felt appalled that things like this were happening to people and people were being ridiculed. I felt bad for having been part of the group that had done the ridiculing. I felt that surely there must be others out there that had seen the creatures I had and there should be information on this out there for them.

Despite my idea to write a book, I couldn't bring myself to do it. I was afraid of these creatures. I felt they were watching me and that they did not *want* me to write a book about this. I didn't know what they would do to me if I were to talk or write about them. I certainly did not want them to come back! The last thing I wanted to do was make these beings angry with me, considering the level of terror I felt when they weren't displeased with me. Fear and a strong sense that these creatures did *not* want me to write a book about the things that I can recall (who knows how many things occurred that I cannot recall) prevented me from sharing these events until now.

I had also felt a sense of wrongness about writing a book about the creatures I've seen. If these beings were spiritual or angels, then it seemed that it wasn't 'right' to write a book about them. I had to analyze my purpose in the writing of a book. Was it to help others or just to have a topic for another book of mine? I have plenty of ideas for books, so it was not necessary for me to write one on my experiences. I wanted to help others; to provide information that I had been unable to find in my search when I was confused and afraid by what I'd experienced.

Despite knowing that I wanted to write the book for a good reason, I still felt uncomfortable about doing so. Again, it all came back to the fact that I didn't feel like I had the 'blessing' of these creatures in regards to writing a book about them. Until I felt that this important aspect had changed, there was no way I was going to write of my experiences.

Besides that, I was and am well aware that my family and friends that do not believe in UFO's or aliens or paranormal events of any kind either will not believe the things I say and avoid me or think I'm crazy.

These were all very good reasons for not broadcasting the things I've experienced that did not fit into the realm of 'normal'.

In March of 2009, I awoke one morning with an overwhelming urge to go to Ecuador. I have a phobia of flying and usually never travel anymore. The urge to go to Ecuador was overpowering and became the top priority in my life. Not only was I terrified of flying, I was a bit afraid of going to South America, was strangely afraid of being in mountains because I always had a creepy feeling that I was being watched while driving in any type of mountain in Nova Scotia, and I had no money to afford such a trip. It didn't help that it was tax time. However, on May 23, 2009, only two months later, I was on my way to South America.

During my six months in the Andes Mountains I lost many of my phobias that had plagued me all my life and gotten worse over the years, including my phobia of fire, electrical fires, heights, walking at night and being alone in a room at night even if there were other people in the house.

Another important fear that disappeared was my fear of writing about my experiences. Not only did I no longer feel it was not right to write of my experiences, but I developed a deep feeling that this was the time for me to write it. A feeling grew that I *am* supposed to write about this and this is the time to do so. I sketched the beings for a couple friends in the Andes Mountains and did not have the same fear that usually accompanied drawing an image of the creatures. Strangely, it also became much easier to talk about the two incidents of seeing the creatures in my adult life.

So, now that I no longer feel that the creatures that have visited me over the years do not want me to write of them, I only have to deal with whatever human criticism will come my way.

I've found that people tend to fall into four groups of listeners. There are those that listen to my story and accept that I have no idea what these beings are. There are those that listen and don't believe I've had these experiences and all of them were dreams. Another group believes I have seen creatures and insist they are aliens. The fourth group insists the creatures are demons.

I don't know if what I've seen are angels, aliens or demons. I don't know if what I've seen really existed or were hallucinations or dreams. Consider this a warning that what you are about to read won't always make sense or be logical. I have no clear conclusions and you may have to form your own conclusions based on your knowledge; I will simply present the facts, including drawings at the end of the book. All I know is that I really experienced these things, in some fashion, and that it is all strange.

CHAPTER TWO

I was an unusual child. I was born prematurely and weighed only 3 lbs. I was always small for my age but very smart. In school, I excelled with honor marks and high scores on IQ tests.

As a child there were strange things that I experienced which my parents wrote off as my over active imagination. Looking back, it could have been the imaginings of a child's mind.... or perhaps not. I really can't tell because I only have my perspective to view this from.

My earliest strange experience was when I was about three years old. I woke up in the back porch. Now that, in itself, is odd because it wasn't like my mother let her three year old out of her sight for however long I had been sleeping in the back porch. What is more, I do not remember going into the back porch before going to sleep.

I awoke on the back porch floor on my knees with my face on my hands; a similar position I've found myself in after fainting as an adult. As a three year old, I would not have known I'd fainted if that were the case then, only that I was waking up. I remember looking up and there was the Friendly Giant, a character from a TV show I watched as a child, so I can see how, when I relayed this to my mother, she thought I'd been dreaming or pretending. Nevertheless, it terrified me.

The giant was not as big as I'd expected the Friendly Giant to be in person, but was only the size of an ordinary man, or even smaller. This was a surprise to me. Looking back and taking into account my small size (at age 5 I was the size of a 3 year old), if I came up to his waist as a three year old, then he would had to have been less than 5 feet tall.

To add to my confusion, the Friendly Giant's trusty sidekick of a puppet was not there. *If that is the friendly giant, then where is Rusty?* It seemed that as soon as I realized confusion in my brain over the absence of the puppet, a smaller creature appeared beside the Friendly Giant. I looked closely at this "puppet" that had suddenly appeared in a bag hanging on the door, very similar to the bag that the Rusty puppet on the TV show was in, but not *exactly* the same.

I was only three years old, but I was not an idiot; I knew that Rusty was only a puppet and someone had their hand in the back of it to animate it. I wondered who was operating this puppet and if he was putting his hand out through the small hole in the woodshed door.

Out of curiosity, I looked closely at the puppet and realized it was *not* a puppet. Even though I do not remember an audible word being spoken, I knew that this creature was alive and wanted me to believe it was a puppet. The creature was small and had big black eyes and was wearing a hooded robe. It was no taller than 24 inches, I think. Because it had been so small, I had been deceived for only a few moments into thinking it was a puppet. I knew that this small giant and creature had been trying to trick me into believing they were the same characters of my favorite TV show.

I stared into its big black eyes and wrinkled face and peered behind it to see if there was a hand coming out of the hole in the woodshed door to prove beyond a doubt that it wasn't a puppet. I didn't see a hand and that confirmed it for me.

It seemed that as soon as I realized that I'd been duped, the demeanor of the giant changed from a friendly one to something else, although I couldn't pinpoint the emotion. He seemed to know that I no longer believed he was the giant from TV. I sensed a feeling of dismay in both the giant and small creature because I did not believe what they wanted me to believe.

I was suddenly afraid of what they would do since I didn't seem to be cooperating with them and I turned and crawled up the steps to the back door. I could not reach the doorknob because I was always very small for my age so I started pounding on the door and screaming and crying for Mom to let me in. She opened the door and was surprised to see me out in the back porch by myself.

Two questions that come to mind are: why didn't my mother see the beings in the back porch and why did they let me go so easily without even physically trying to stop me?

"How did you get out there?" My mother demanded, grabbing me by the arm and pulling me inside. I could not stop crying long enough to explain what happened and her tolerance for a screaming three year old was very low. I apparently screamed and cried for 15 minutes (as she has told this) and only eventually stopped screaming when she threatened to give me "something to cry for"; namely a spanking. Throughout my adult life she reminded me many times of running in the house from somewhere and standing in the middle of the floor and just crying nonstop for about an hour. I don't remember doing that except for the incident involving the Friendly Giant. Maybe I chose not to remember or maybe I just can't remember the other times. Whatever the case, my mother often reminded me of how I often ran in the house and just stood in the middle of the floor crying and screaming for an hour and I wouldn't shut up.

On this particular incident, once I was calm enough to explain what happened, she insisted I had just had a dream. I remember making her go out in the back porch with me to *see* for herself. I could prove it to her that I was telling the truth. It seemed that it took a long time to convince her to go into the back porch with me and when she finally did, there was no one there.

Now, keep in mind, I was only three years old. Perhaps I *was* just dreaming. A three year old can likely not tell the difference between a dream and reality when they wake up. But my problem with being able to come to a firm opinion on what I experienced is this: WHY would a three year old be sleeping in the back porch alone with the house door closed? Mom never let me out of her sight when I was that small.   My second question was *how* on Earth did I possibly get into the back porch since I was way too small to reach the doorknob?

I don't know what that experience really was, though. A dream? An encounter with an alien in disguise? The wild imagination of a three year old?

When I was small, and perhaps because of that incident in the porch, I was afraid of the dark and afraid to be outside alone. I had unusual fears for a child, I think. If I was outside playing and an airplane flew overhead I would run into the house. Even to this day, I feel an unexplainable fear when I see airplanes or helicopters overhead if I'm outside alone.

When I was a small child I was very spiritual. I said my prayers every night and *knew* there was a God. I wasn't a child that suspected there was a god or doubted there was a god; I knew beyond a shadow of a doubt there was one.

When I was five and started school, my greatest joy was receiving a little red testament at school. I carried it everywhere with me. When I was still five, I begged Mom to let me get baptized and begged her to call the local Baptist minister and ask him to baptize me. She didn't do so right away and I begged her for weeks. Finally she told him that I wished to be baptized and arranged a meeting for me with him. She took me to his house and I remember standing in front of him and I could tell by the look on his face he was not going to agree to baptize me. Looking back now, I can completely understand that. I was five years old and looked like I was three.

He asked why I wanted to be baptized.

"Because I want to serve God and want to live my life for God," I explained as I stood in front of him. "I belong to God and I want to give my life to him."

After many questions and a lengthy discussion, he eventually agreed to baptize me. I cannot remember the entire discussion or what I actually said that changed his mind, but when we left his house he was convinced that I had a right to be baptized. A few weeks later I was joining adults at the edge of a river and was baptized in water that came up to the minister's knees.

Whether my strong desire to be baptized had to do with the fact that my mother took me to church a lot as a kid, or whatever caused me to run in the house and stand and cry for long periods of time, or my constant fear of dying as a child, I don't know.

I remember that all during my childhood I was afraid to go to sleep and would cry for hours into the night. I always battled a strong feeling that if I went to sleep, there was a strong possibility of dying before I woke up. I don't think it is normal for a little kid to experience this every night when they go to bed. I remember lying in bed and staring at the ceiling, being so afraid of going to sleep and crying for hours. Nighttime was horrific for me because of this overwhelming feeling I was going to die before morning. This lasted up until my teen years. I did experience this as young as five years old so perhaps that had a lot to do with my demand to get baptized; I wanted to make sure I could get into heaven if I *did* die in the night.

Strange experiences continued to happen to me as a child. Every now and then I would feel like I'd just 'come back' from somewhere.

One day I suddenly "came back" or became present outside standing by my pedal car. I had no memory of getting outside, just of suddenly having the feeling of being 'put back' there. I suddenly became aware of everything around me and saw our next-door neighbor crossing the road to come over to visit my mother. I remember running from the pedal car across the front lawn to grab her hand because I was so scared.

I had no memory of anything previous to finding myself standing by my pedal car at the end of our driveway. I also would have never played even as far as the driveway by myself, even though the driveway was near the house. I never felt safe outside the house.

This strange phenomenon continued to happen to me throughout my childhood. I had no control over these incidents and eventually began to recognize a strange feeling just before they occurred. I cannot explain the feeling except that it was a sudden sense of fear and foreboding accompanied by a thought of *Oh no! It's going to happen again!*

After each experience like this I was left with strange images in my mind. Images that would just stick in my mind . Images that made no sense to me. One was of a growing bubble-type thing that had ropes all around it to contain it. I cannot explain it well enough so I've included a sketch of it in the back of the book. The best way to imagine what I saw is this: imagine bread dough rising but being surrounded by crossing ropes; the dough would rise around the ropes and keep expanding. That was what I was seeing, some sort of substance expanding. I have no idea what this image was. It was always in my head just after these 'away' experiences. Later on in life I had the beginning stages of cervical cancer which my doctor described as a cluster of cells that looked like grapes that were growing; perhaps they looked like that unexplainable image that had been in my head so often as a child. Maybe I somehow had the image in my head of molecular chains, or something. I really don't know since it started when I was such a small child and at that time I had no 'real world' knowledge to link the image to.

Other images that stuck in my head were hieroglyphic type symbols. This created an interest in me of ancient Egyptians and archaeology and I would spend hours of my childhood watching every excavation and archaeological show that came on our two-channel TV back in the early 70's.

In my adult life I actually remember having a dream (which I remembered to be a dream and had no confusion over thinking it was a real incident and I was awake) in which I was standing by this huge stone that had hieroglyphic carvings in it and I was able to read it perfectly. The sign, by the way, said this: *The Brothers of Atlantis must live by the laws of Atlantis.* This had such a profound impact on me emotionally when I woke up that I'm in the process of writing a fictional novel based around this called Brothers Of Atlantis that will be published in the spring of 2010.

I also had a keen interest in UFO's and science fiction from a very young age as well as a fear of UFO's and anything that was flying overhead. A helicopter or airplane evoked as much fear in me as if it were a UFO and I'd run for the house as fast as my little legs would carry me. It might also be a little strange that I had this interest since when I was a small child I don't think there was that much information out on the subject. I was born in 1964 so in the late 60's and early 70's, I don't think that I had any access to actual information on the subject. My father likely recounted his experiences of seeing UFO's at that time, though.

These 'away' episodes only ever happened when I was alone and so I became afraid to be alone. I would not go outside to play unless my brother went with me. I wouldn't even go into the back porch (which I avoided for years) alone without my brother.

As I grew older, these experiences, or episodes happened less and less often. To this day I have no idea what they were, whether they were some kind of brain glitch, such as a type of seizure, or if they were alien abductions, or something else. I have no explanations, only my perception of the experiences. When I became an adult, the experiences stopped nearly altogether, or at least my awareness of them.

One of the experiences that sticks in my memory today is of when I was about 15 years old. I don't remember anything that happened before the incident, but I remember 'coming back' and suddenly becoming aware of being in my bedroom lying on my bed. At that moment of awareness I remember also having an immediate memory of a swift whooshing sound and being above the trees beside our house. I remembered the sensation of coming down very fast, not falling, but deliberate movement downward from the sky, faster than the speed of light I guess. It was a tremendous rushing experience as if my entire body was suddenly shoved through an alternate dimension and into my bedroom. I had an actual memory of coming right through the wall. I remember, as strange as it sounds, moving between the fibers in the wall. I remember moving between the various layers of the wall so fast that I couldn't mentally process it but was able to retain the cutaway type image of the wall. At the time, I had no words to describe this, only confusion and fear. My high IQ and ample common sense kept me from sharing this with anyone at the time; I knew that no one would believe me. It was even more than I could process at that time!

As soon as I realized I was in my room, I looked around me but everything looked strange and unfamiliar. It was as if I were from another planet. I heard my mother and sister talking in the kitchen but I couldn't understand what they were saying. I could not understand English. I listened to them babble back and forth to each other as I reaffirmed in my mind "that is my sister....that is my mother". But then, I had to completely analyze what the words mother and sister even meant, and what human relationships really were. I suddenly found it strange that people grouped themselves together in 'families' and every little group lived in different houses and ate together and considered themselves to be more or less owned by each other.

My mind scrambled to understand my human condition. All kinds of seemingly new information were flooding my brain. We lived in a family...what is family? What does that word mean? I rolled the word around in my head over and over but it made no sense. I looked around me at the walls of my bedroom and they seemed so strange. It was odd to me during those few moments that houses were made out of wood and I realized that wooden walls are not solid even though they appear to be. I considered at that moment how silly it was to build houses to protect us when the walls weren't even solid. Years later, after researching quantum physics I discovered that my perceptions at that time were correct; a wooden wall really is not solid on a subatomic level.

After a few moments, the language being spoken in the kitchen by my mother and sister became discernable to me and within five minutes I was completely fluent in English again. I know this all sounds really weird and like some sort of seizure or something. At the time I could not find the words to describe it to my mother so I kept it to myself. I thought for sure I was going crazy. I had no idea what was happening to me but it was scary and I wished and prayed that it would stop.

Today I have no solid conclusions as to what those experiences were. At one end of the spectrum of possibilities I think I could have had some weird type of seizures. I never told my parents about this at the time and so was never tested for this. I always had the feeling that this was not something I should talk about. I don't know whether I got that feeling from early on in childhood with my mother insisting my odd experiences were dreams, or if there were other reasons for it. As an adult, however, I was tested several times for seizures in an attempt to find answers but these tests always revealed that my brain was perfectly fine.

If aliens or interdimensional entities were abducting me which is the possibility at the other end of the spectrum, then perhaps they ingrained in me the need to not tell others. Whether I cannot remember what happened during the time before I had the 'coming back' experience because my memory of the event was erased or because it was just too traumatic for me to be able to deal with it, I have no memories of ever being actually abducted by anything; only the symptoms.

Whether these strange goings-on in my childhood was the cause or result of my desire to be close to God and want to learn everything about God and supernatural historical events, I have no clue. If I were being abducted, were the abductors in any way related to the God or angels of the bible? What were the strange beings that had visited me at least once in my back porch?

Whether my closeness to God was inspired by whatever visitations I was experiencing or a direct result of the unremembered fear, I tried to stay as close to God as possible. When I was a small child, I knew the 10 commandments and worked at keeping them. When I was 12, I insisted on going to Youth Group even though at that time my mother was not going to any church. I went to Sunday school and church services alone, even though my parents did not go. As a teen I never drank, smoked, partied, did drugs or had sex. I had a very strong sense of right and wrong and an over-sensitive aversion to anything resembling 'wrong'. Not only did I not drink or do drugs, I would not be friends with kids that did. There was no amount of peer pressure from boyfriends that was strong enough to make me have sex during my teens. No amount of peer pressure was strong enough for me to smoke, drink or do drugs.

I've also never been able to watch TV shows or movies with violence in them. Swearing, anger, murder, or any depiction of evil invoked such a strong sense of evil in my gut that I have to avoid it. If I'm watching a movie that is very interesting, or even a documentary, and a commercial that comes on advertising immoral videos, I feel an overbearing sense of 'wrong' with a physical pain in my stomach and have to turn the channel, refusing to support a network that has immoral sponsors.

I've always been keenly aware when I was being lied to. I learned over the years to trust that intuition and I've never been wrong. I've also had a very low tolerance level for stupidity.

I have a distinct aversion to entertainment based around violence, sex, vampires, mummies, murder, death, ghosts, evil spirits, demons, etc. I gravitate towards shows and documentaries of a scientific nature, especially quantum physics, cymatics, time travel and astronomy. Cymatics is the study of how sound waves manipulate matter. Different frequencies can create different geometric patterns in sand, water or iron filings or other material. I am firmly convinced that crop circles are made solely with the use of sound.

The small creature in a hooded robe that visited me in my back porch when I was three was to visit me, with others like him, two more times during the course of my life prior to the writing of this book. I will go into detail about these visits later in the book. I cannot say whether they will return, or if they do more often than I'm aware of and just have no memory of it. The times I do remember were so frightening that I have absolutely no desire to be hypnotized to find out.

I also have no idea what these creatures are or what to actually call them. Creatures are what I've been calling them. Whether they are angels, watchers, demons, spirits, or aliens, I really don't know. The only thing I know for a fact is that they are strange creatures.

CHAPTER THREE

I think it's only fair to include, to the best of my ability, my parents' experiences as well, as well as to mention that my first experience at 3 years old with the Friendly Giant and a small hooded creature in my back porch happened in 1967 which was the same year as the Shag Harbour incident.

The Shag Harbour incident is Canada's Roswell. In October of 1967 many people witnessed strange lights in the sky. One of these 'crashed' into Shag Harbour. The military, police, fire department and fishermen were all gathered to search for bodies and debris of what they supposed was a plane crash in the harbor that night. However, no such debris was found and a three-day observation of a strange light under the water culminated in the strange light surfacing on the third day and then zooming off into the sky.

I am not going to write all the details about that incident since there is ample information on the Internet for anyone who looks, including videos on Youtube from the History channel that provide detailed information of that incident. If the reader has further interest in this, let him look up this incident on his own.

This chapter is designated to discuss my parents' encounters in as much as they were relayed to me. They may have had more experiences that they did not tell me about, but I will relate what they did tell.

When my father was 14 years old he was biking home one night from his grandmother's house. He saw a UFO in the sky go down behind some trees that were quite near him. When he relayed this to me I asked him if he went into the woods to see the UFO close up.

"No way!" he exclaimed, his eyes wide as he displayed his fear of that incident. "I headed for home as fast as my legs would peddle!"

His reaction confirmed for me that he was telling the truth. If he'd been just trying to entertain me with a story, he would have gone on to describe his encounter in a much more entertaining way...instead he took off as fast as he could.

The second time he saw a UFO, he was walking home on the dirt road I lived on as a child, carrying my older sister who was three at the time. He saw a UFO in the sky and pointed to it. When I asked my sister if she remembers seeing a UFO when she was three, she said she remembers the incident, but did not see the UFO.

She was only three and remembers him pointing at the sky and saying, "Look, there's a flying saucer! Three of them!" She has told me she looked around but at her young age was looking for an actual saucer like she'd seen on the table and was too little to understand what he was pointing at, so she did not manage to see it.

Those are the only two incidents that my father told me of, perhaps he had more, I do not know.

My mother only told me of one strange incident in her life, that I could remember. She said when she was about 9 or 10 years old, she had a strange dream that she got up, went out in the orchard in the middle of the night to pick apples and there was someone there (I can't remember her description of this being, or even if he was human). I cannot remember the altercation she had with this being, but I do remember she said she was punching him, trying to get away. In the morning, she awoke underneath her bed on the floor with a bunch of apples and a nosebleed.

Did aliens, with perhaps an implant that caused a nosebleed, abduct my mother? Or did she just sleepwalk to the orchard and somehow punch herself in the nose, causing it to bleed, and then return to her room, choosing to sleep underneath her bed with the apples she'd collected?

There are so many ways I could interpret this, but the only things I really know are the facts as she told them. It was obvious she had gone out to the orchard; the apples were the evidence. There had been some kind of altercation, even if she only punched herself in the nose, since she woke up with a nosebleed. Why could she remember getting up and going to the orchard but not remember coming back from the orchard? Why was she underneath her bed when she woke up? Was she hiding from someone or something? Had she just been sleepwalking and somehow missed her bed upon return? Had she been abducted by a UFO and beings that put her back in the wrong place when they returned her? I have no idea what really happened and was certainly not there. I can only recount her story with absolutely no conclusions of my own for it.

Sadly, both of my parents are gone now and I am unable to get clarification on any of these questions I have. When my father was on his deathbed, he told me again of his UFO sighting when he was 14.

The only thing I do know is that my parents had strange experiences and I had strange experiences. None of my siblings recall strange experiences. It makes me wonder, why me? Why am I the only one that saw creatures when I was a child, had strange 'absences', and continued to have strange occurrences in my adult life? Did the others also have these but just don't remember or know it? Or am I the only one? And why? Why me? So many questions, so few answers.

CHAPTER FOUR

By 1993, after two divorces, I was left alone to raise three sons. Although I had never fully decided on what the strange experiences of 'absences' I'd had as a child were, I had never in any way connected them to alien abductions or anything of that nature. It had just always been a strange and scary thing that occasionally happened to me when I was alone during my childhood. This instilled a fear of being alone in me. Nothing of any similar significance that I could recall happened between those years and 1993.

In 1993, I was driving to Annapolis from Digby with a friend of mine. Annapolis is a 20-minute drive from Digby, with the Bear River exit only about 10 minutes from Digby. The strange thing is that we left Digby and drove for what felt like over a half hour and still hadn't reached the Bear River exit. The sky was a strange purple hue that was unlike anything I'd ever seen before. I began to get worried because we should have reached the Bear River exit ages ago and should have been to Annapolis by that point but we didn't seem to be anywhere I recognized.

"Did we pass the Bear River exit?" I asked my friend in the car. I thought that maybe I somehow had been oblivious to passing it while we were talking.

"No," he said in a concerned tone. "We should have reached it by now."

"Doesn't everything look strange to you?" I asked, hoping I wasn't sounding weird.

"Yeah," he agreed. "And how come there are no telephone poles?"

Once he pointed that out I felt a strange sense of awareness. We were traveling on a highway that usually had electricity lines, phone lines, etc. There were no utility poles anywhere.

"And we haven't passed another car since we left town," I pointed out.

There was not another vehicle anywhere on the road as far as we could see in either direction, no utility poles, no exits and no houses or buildings in sight.

"Maybe we should just turn around," I suggested, trying not to panic.

"I think we should," he agreed. He didn't mask his alarm very well and that did nothing to make me feel the least bit safe.

I turned the car around and headed back towards home. We had been driving for over 30 minutes, yet once we turned the car around we were back in Digby within 10 minutes. Neither of us could explain nor understand what had just happened but since we reached Digby safely we decided to make a second attempt to drive to Annapolis.

I turned the car around again and headed back towards Annapolis. We passed the Bear River exit in the expected 10-minute time frame and reached Annapolis in 30 minutes. I have no idea to this day what had happened the first time. It was the strangest driving experience I'd ever had to this day and nothing like that has ever happened again.

In January of 1997, my two oldest boys turned 8 and 10 years old. On that year we had decided at the first of the year that on each of our birthdays in that year, rather than have a big party, we would go on a spending spree with each child getting $100 to spend. Nick's birthday was on January 17th and so we spent $400 on a shopping spree at Toys R Us in Halifax. On the 30th, it was my oldest son's 10th birthday and we were heading to Yarmouth for another spending spree, with each of the kids and myself having $100 to spend.

Being in the winter in Nova Scotia, sunset came early, somewhere around 5:30pm. Yarmouth is an hour and a half drive away. We'd left Digby around 5pm when my ex picked us up to drive us. It was nearing 6:30pm when we were close to Yarmouth and it was dark. As we were driving we suddenly saw three large strange lights in the sky ahead of us, slowly and silently moving across the sky, equidistant apart like three full moons.

"Those can't be planes," I said to my ex.

"No, those aren't planes," he said. This alarmed me because he is a skeptic when it comes to UFO's.

"Do you think they're UFO's?" I asked, fully expecting him to assure me they weren't.

"I don't know," he said. Now this phrase alarmed me most. My ex is a guy that knows everything about everything and is always right and never wrong. I've never heard him utter the phrase 'I don't know' about *anything* ever in my life!

"You should pull over so we can watch them," I said, afraid that he would go in the ditch or something while staring at the sky.

Amazingly (he has never listened to me before in his life, which is mainly why he was an ex!) he pulled over and turned off the car. He is also the kind of guy that won't pull over for anything; time is money and every moment he wastes drives him crazy. When we would go somewhere there were no detours or stops of any kind.

I didn't feel fear at seeing these lights because they were only lights, not solid objects and at the time I didn't *know* they were UFO's (I still don't *know* what we saw). I wasn't afraid of lights, especially as long as they kept moving. If they'd suddenly changed direction, then I likely would have been freaked out, but as it was, they just steadily and silently moved across the sky. I couldn't tell their altitude but they seemed to be just slightly above the trees. They were three large round white lights, similar to three full moons, all gliding equidistant apart. The distance between them was considerable and I perceived them as three separate objects, not just three lights on one object. They were also in a straight line across, not in a triangle formation or anything. I've put a CGI image in the back of the book to show exactly what I saw.

I thought the lights were unusual as I'd never seen anything similar before, but this was also before I began researching UFO's in earnest and realized that lights in the sky were common with alien abductions.

I don't think we had any contact with aliens or anything on that night. I wasn't keeping track of time and don't know if there was missing time involved in that evening or not. Nothing seemed to be out of the ordinary, anyway, after the lights were gone. We just restarted the car and continued our drive to Yarmouth, although after seeing those lights I had lost interest in shopping and couldn't wait to get back home. I've asked my kids if they remember seeing the lights that night and none of them remember it. They do, however, remember the incident of pulling over in the car and me talking with my ex about the lights, but they do not recall seeing the lights themselves.

Later that year, sometime in the summer, I awoke to find strange creatures on my bed. I always slept with the hall light on so the kids could see if they went to the bathroom in the night. That was the official explanation, but in reality, I'd felt the need to sleep with a hallway light on all my life; I was always afraid of the dark. The hallway light being on is what made it possible to see these creatures clearly in the night.

I awakened to the feeling of a heavy weight on me. I opened my eyes and in the dim light I saw a brown hooded creature sitting on top of me. It was about two feet tall. I'm not sure if it was sitting or standing since its brown, hooded, monk-like robe completely covered its body. The weight of it held me down and I looked at the phone on my nightstand and was going to call my ex to come up. But as soon as I thought of calling someone, I became paralyzed from my neck down. I could still turn my head but my arms were under the blanket by my side and there was no way I could move with the weight of this creature on me.

I was terrified. The knowledge that there are beings that can get into your house despite locked doors and windows was very unnerving. The creatures were clearly not of this world or dimension. I am not saying they were from outer space, but they were clearly not of this dimension.

I was traumatized and had never felt fear like that before in my life. I stared into the huge round black eyes and I remember thinking that this certainly couldn't be an alien encounter because anything I'd ever read about aliens only ever mentioned slanted eyes, gray skin and nothing about big round black eyes and brown monk robes! I never got the feeling they were the aliens I'd read about that abducted people and took them aboard UFO's and experimented on them. These beings never gave me that impression at all. These were something worse, from another dimension.

Nothing I'd ever read in my life had prepared me for this being. At that time, I had not remembered the first time I'd seen a creature like this in my back porch. After so many years of being told it was a dream as a child, I'd done my best to forget it. As far as I could tell at this time, this was the first time I was seeing such a creature. The big black eyes were surrounded by many wrinkles, above and below the eyes. The wrinkles continued down the sides of the cheeks, giving the creature the appearance of being very, very old. Older than any human being I'd ever seen. I felt like it was thousands of years old. The nose and mouth were small, but humanlike. This shocked me because I'd never read anything about alien creatures having human noses.

I stared at the brown hooded robe the being was wearing and I wanted to feel it to see if it really was burlap, which is what it appeared to be. It looked as ancient as the creature in it.

I moved my head a little to the left as movement caught my eye. There were two more of these beings on my bed, and two in the hallway scooting across the floor toward my sons' room. I was alarmed that the one on me was holding me down while there were two creatures heading towards my kids. I had no idea what they were going to do to my kids but I felt like they were there for the purpose of doing something to my kids and the ones on my bed were there for the purpose of keeping me from going to my kids.

The beings didn't make any sounds, but when they moved, they moved so fast that they left visual trails behind them. They moved faster than my eyes could follow. They zipped across the hallway and I could only clearly see them when they stopped. It was like when I looked at them they froze and stood still for a moment.

I looked back at the creature on me and I was so terrified it is a miracle I didn't have a heart attack. I was so alarmed and concerned about what the creatures were doing to my kids, or going to do to my kids. Whether it was for my benefit or theirs, the creature on me reached towards me with a silver wand and touched my forehead with it. I didn't even feel the touch of it before I was out. It apparently was a device to put me to sleep.

I awoke some time later, thinking, 'whew, that was some dream! It was so real!"

Then I realized I couldn't move and I opened my eyes and the creature was still on top of me. It must have only been a few seconds I'd been out because the creatures in the hall were still in the hall. Maybe being touched with the wand hadn't been to put me to sleep; perhaps I'd just fainted in fear.

I felt a panic rise up in me as I realized it was real and hadn't been a dream. As I started to panic, the creature sitting on me reached forward with the silver wand again and I was out as it touched my forehead.

I woke up for the third time, some time later, afraid to open my eyes in case they were still there. I could feel the weight still on me, so I opened my eyes slowly and the creature was still on me and there were two out in the hallway and the other two must have been in the room with the kids.

The panic I felt was unbelievable as I realized that this was a very real thing and these creatures were not leaving any time soon. I was totally immobilized and I had no idea what these creatures wanted or would do to me and my family. I was so scared I could not breathe. The being sitting on me reached forward with the silver wand for the third time and I was out.

Some time later, I didn't know how much later, I woke up again and did not dare to open my eyes. I was afraid they would still be there, but it didn't feel like the weight of the creature was still on me so I slowly opened my eyes. I was overcome with a sense of relief as I realized the beings were gone and it was beginning to get light outside.

I jumped out of bed and ran to the kids' room next door to check on them. They were all sleeping soundly, alive and okay.

I ran back to my room and called my ex, explaining all the events of the night, but he insisted it was a dream and nothing to worry about.

I do not know who or what those creatures were, where they were from or what they wanted or did, but I do know they were real and this was *not* a dream! I was frustrated by not being believed. I called my sister but she also believed it was just a dream. I decided I better stop telling people if I didn't want people to think I was insane.

I was thankful the creatures were gone and it was daytime. Everything always seemed better in the light of day.

I felt so guilty over not taking my middle son's claims that monsters were on his bed when he was two. He was now eight years old and we'd turned their bedroom into a boys campout with their mattresses and box springs directly on the floor to remove the 'under the bed' where monsters could hide. When Nick had been two he had claimed numerous times of monsters on his bed at night and I didn't believe him. I now knew what it felt like when no one believed that I'd seen creatures on my bed. I was alarmed that these were probably the same monsters my son had seen.

I was plagued with insomnia after that. I was too fearful to go to sleep at night and for a long time ended up falling asleep in exhaustion with my bedroom lamp on. I was too afraid to sleep alone.

Although I stayed up most nights out of fear, the creatures never visited me again while I lived in that house; at least not that I was aware of. It would be close to ten years before I saw these creatures again.

The strange thing was, since that incident with those creatures I began to have prophetic or psychic dreams. I would have detailed dreams about various things that would play out in real life exactly as they had in the dreams. Two days before the space shuttle crash, I dreamed it and saw the explosion in the sky exactly as it showed on TV two days later.

I had psychic dreams in which relatives requested my help with explanations of facts that I'd never known, and within several months I would receive a phone call with the exact request and explanation word for word. I had dreams involving my sister and her boyfriend and the date they would be reunited when she thought she would never see him again. I had a prophetic dream about my boyfriend and I breaking up and the scenario played out exactly as it had in my dream less than a week later.

Whether these prophetic dreams were a result of whatever that silver wand was that was touched to my forehead, I have no idea. I do not remember ever having any prophetic dreams before that incident and as far as I can tell, they only began occurring after that. It may have had nothing to do at all with the silver wand. That wand may have just been a device to put me to sleep. Or it may have done something to my brain. I have no idea; I'm just guessing here. I'm not writing this book from the viewpoint of an expert on this subject, but only as an experiencer of these things. I'm not trying to give others answers, but rather to let others that have experienced similar things in their lives realize they are not alone.

By 2006, I had moved to a house outside of town. My father was in the final stages of his battle with throat cancer and spent 7 weeks in the hospital. During those 7 weeks, my days consisted of rushing back and forth to the hospital to sit with my father because he could go any time. Sometimes the kids went with me, sometimes stayed at friends' houses or with other relatives. It was summer so there was no school.

Because every day I was told that my father might only have hours left to live, supper consisted of fast food via a drive through. 7 weeks of this kind of lifestyle, accompanied by the stress of my father's condition as well as the stress of my boss who became less and less understanding of my work absences as the weeks drew on, were taking a toll on me. My feet were swelling pretty badly but I ignored it because I was so preoccupied with my father's condition. My feet were swollen constantly and were beginning to frighten me, but I didn't really think it was anything serious.

After my father passed away in July of 2006, and his funeral was over, I was exhausted and sick, as well as grieving. In August, my feet remained swollen but now it had spread up my legs and there was even swelling in my lower back. I felt nauseated and exhausted all the time. I went to the doctor and he ordered tests. His conclusion was that I had chronic renal failure and high blood pressure; my kidneys had failed and the toxins which were now not being filtered out by my kidneys were seeping into the tissues of my feet and legs, causing swelling and slowly poisoning my body. By the time I went to the doctor I hadn't been able to urinate in about two days and hadn't been able to eat in a week or drink water even in a couple of days. With my aversion to doctors and hospitals, I didn't actually go to my doctor until I actually felt like I was dying.

My doctor told me that I basically had two options; dialysis or kidney transplant. In my weakened and ill state he wanted to admit me to the hospital, but I refused and said I wanted to go home to pray about it. I didn't feel comfortable with my blood being taken out of my body to be cleaned or someone else's organs being put inside me. I needed to go home and think and pray and I was feeling so sick and miserable, I just wanted to go home. He stressed the importance of dialysis and how serious this was, but all I wanted to do was go home.

I went home and contacted every single person I knew in my family and on the Internet, told them my health problem and asked everyone to pray for me.

I had a fever, I couldn't eat or drink anything and couldn't use the bathroom. I felt like I was dying. I spent the rest of the day in bed, exhausted and ill and got up periodically to email people asking them to pray for me, make sure the boys ate, emailed my boss explaining I was sick, etc. I made it to bed for the night early and quickly drifted off to sleep, laying on my right side.

A short time later I awoke and saw something move by my right outstretched hand. I thought it was the cat at first, but almost instantly realized it was not a cat and a feeling of fear and dread washed over me and I just knew *they* were back. I looked at the small creature sitting beside my hand and in the dim light I could see a small black skinned creature with huge black eyes wearing a brown monk-like hooded robe sitting beside my hand.

I knew already that there were more on my bed and I turned my head and peered over my shoulder. I was still laying on my right side. I could hear my heart pounding in my ears as I was engulfed in panic. There were two similar creatures sitting behind my back and two at the foot of the bed in front of me.

Despite my fear I remember trying to calm myself by thinking *"I'm just sick…I have a really high fever. I'm just hallucinating."* It would have been very believable for me to think that. The room was spinning, I knew I had a fever and I realized how sick I was.

Even trying to convince myself that this was a hallucination did nothing to ease my mind and my panic increased when I felt their bony fingers touch me. The two in front of me on the bed had moved up by my hips and were massaging my abdomen with their bony fingers while the two behind me were massaging my back where my kidneys were. Their bony fingers hurt and the pain got increasingly worse as their fingers massaged right into my body, through the skin and muscle until their hands were inside my body massaging my kidneys directly. It felt like knives were being shoved into my body.

The pain was excruciating and I writhed in pain as I wished for them to stop. I was so terrified and traumatized I couldn't even scream, but just moan in pain. When I tried to scream nothing came out. But then I heard them make noises. At the time I assumed they were communicating with each other, because it was certainly not for my benefit. They did not seem the least bit concerned that I was in excruciating pain and fear. They just kept massaging my kidneys as if it were some assignment they had to complete.

Meanwhile, as they massaged and made strange sounds, the fifth creature still sat beside my right arm, although he had moved closer to me now. He was sitting no more than a few inches from my face. I saw that he had many wrinkles above and below his huge round black eyes. Again, the feeling I had was that I was looking at a very ancient creature. The wrinkles circled his eyes numerous times and then fell in vertical wrinkles down his aged cheeks on either side of his tiny human-like mouth and nose. For a split second as I stared at his eyes and many wrinkles, I felt a strange sense of humanness about him. For a moment I stopped thinking of these beings, the one I was looking at particularly, as being scary creatures but as being something more. I felt I was face to face with an ancient being that had seen many thousands of generations of humans. In that one moment of an absence of fear, I felt the being I was face to face with was always there, perhaps with a duty to watch over me . . . *us*. Maybe these were what were known as the Watchers, perhaps guardian angels.

The four continued to massage as I suffered in unbearable pain. Their voices sounded like high-pitched whale sounds; a screeching kind of series of noises. It was loud, painful and terrifying.

At the time I remember thinking *I'm hearing into another dimension.* Their sounds had an echo to them.

When my heart was pounding so loud in my ears and my terror was beyond belief, they suddenly stopped and I passed out, or vice versa. All I know is that I had a moment of unconsciousness.

I awoke again in what felt like only a few moments and thought, *whew, thank god that was only a dream!* But then I saw the creature beside my hand move and I suddenly knew that it hadn't been a dream no matter how much I wanted it to be. I looked slowly and sure enough, the other four were still there, two in front of me and two behind me. I felt panic, more so at the knowledge that this was *not* a dream after all. It was as though they had stopped for a moment out of kindness or compassion since the experience was so traumatic for me.

Again, the four surrounding me began massaging my abdomen, and then I heard their high-pitched squealing noises, and they massaged into my abdomen, working on my kidneys. Whereas at that time, I assumed they were just talking among themselves, not caring how traumatized I was, I now think that perhaps they were using those sounds to influence the material makeup of my physical body that allowed them to put their hands right through my skin with no surgical equipment, although it felt like knives cutting through me.

I writhed in pain and fear until it was unbearable, both physically and emotionally, and they stopped, allowing me to rest in a temporary sleep for a few minutes. Then, again, I woke up, saw the creature by my hand, saw the others, felt them, heard them, and then another break.

Each time I woke up, it was with dread that this was not a dream and these creatures were here. Each time they were absolutely still as I woke up, then I saw them, then felt them massage my kidneys, then heard them. The pain was excruciating.

This cycle continued about ten times and in the morning I awoke, exhausted and traumatized; afraid to open my eyes. When I finally worked up the courage to open my eyes I was relieved that it was light outside and the creatures were nowhere to be seen.

I got out of the bed as quickly as I could, thankful that I had been apparently unharmed and could move. During the ordeal with the creatures I was not sure whether it was fear that prevented me from moving or if they had paralyzed me somehow. Perhaps the one creature that sat beside my arm the entire time was there to keep me paralyzed, or perhaps it was their sounds that did that trick. I had no clue.

Even before I felt totally safe that I was alone in my room, I had to go use the bathroom. This was a strange feeling since I had been unable to use the bathroom for days. I was amazed that my kidneys were apparently working again!

Over the long weekend, I was able to drink water and use the bathroom and the toxins drained out of my body. When I went back to the hospital on Tuesday for another blood test, I was feeling much better and my kidneys seemed to be working. The tests showed that my kidneys were indeed working now and my doctor was amazed. When I asked him how this was possible when on Friday he had told me that it was impossible for kidney function to be restored, he just shook his head and said it was possibly a misdiagnosis on his part.

I didn't tell him about the creatures. I didn't tell anyone for a long time. I still didn't have a clear understanding of what had actually happened.

I was traumatized and confused. How could these creatures possibly be real? If they were real, where did they come from and how had they gotten into my room? I did not, on any of the occasions I've seen them, see any UFO's or lights in the sky. I have seen lights and objects in the sky, but those were on totally separate occasions and I had no experiences with creatures when I'd seen the lights or the object.

Despite the fact that this was the third time I'd seen these same brown creatures with hooded robes on, I was still no closer to figuring out what was going on. My kidneys had not been working on Friday. Friday night strange creatures massaged my kidneys all night and by Saturday morning my kidneys were working again. By

Tuesday, the swelling had significantly gone down in my legs and feet.

I still have to be careful with my kidneys; if I get too cold, they hurt, if I eat too much sugar, they hurt.

I decided that these creatures must be angels or something. If not, then why – on a night that every person was praying for me – did they show up? They did not harm me; in fact they healed me, apparently. They were obviously not of this dimension and I heard them speak in a manner that was obviously not of this earth.

I was so traumatized, I did not even tell my kids about this. I didn't want them to feel unsafe in their own home and feel that there were creatures that had the ability to get into our home in the middle of the night with our doors and windows secured.

I thought either I hallucinated the entire thing and my kidneys started working coincidentally, or I hallucinated the whole thing and my doctor had made a misdiagnosis, or my kidneys had failed and when everyone that knew me prayed for me, God sent angels to heal me and they did.

My sisters and friends were amazed at my recovery and I simply told them that angels came in the night and healed me. I left it at that, I didn't want to tell them the scary details and at that time I was so frustrated if people didn't believe me. I had tried to speak of the first time in my adult life I'd seen these creatures on my bed and anyone that had never seen anything like this wrote it off as being nothing more than a vivid dream.

I don't know about most people, but I have no trouble distinguishing that I am waking up when I'm waking up in the morning, and no trouble realizing that I've had a dream or two in the night. This was not like that; it was *not* a matter of me just *thinking* I was waking up.

Regardless, I was left distressed and traumatized by the events of that night, although always thankful that my kidney function had been restored.

About a year later, after I was with my current partner, I had a strange dream. I dreamed that I was in this circular white room that was a strange type of medical examination room. I was sitting on a stool and a doctor was standing behind me running a strange type of scanner over my body checking my organs. I could not see the doctor, I was only aware that he was standing behind me with this hand-held scanner running it slowly over my back.

He held it behind my lower back and on a glass medical table in the center of the room, a 3D model or hologram of my kidney appeared turning slowly in a clockwise direction on the table. I knew I was looking at my kidney and could see that it was a living organ. I was amazed at this technology and could not figure out how my kidney could be outside my body lying on this glass table. Then the doctor moved the scanner, reaching around my left side and holding it over my stomach. I saw my stomach laying on the glass table ahead of me. Then I saw my liver laying on the table. It was all black. The doctor told me this is what was happening to my liver from drinking Diet Coke and I needed to quit drinking it because it was damaging my stomach and liver. I've included a sketch of this at the back of the book.

That is all I remember of my dream, but I found it to be a strange dream and it scared me into trying to give up Diet Coke.

CHAPTER FIVE

Plagued by the need for answers I read every book on UFO's I could find, researched on the Internet for small brown hooded creatures but apparently I was the only person in the entire world that has seen them, or maybe I didn't research it well enough; I don't know. But I've been seeking answers since my first encounters with the strange creatures, desperately seeking anyone else who has seen them as well. In the process I learned a lot about screen memories, lost time and blocked memories. This has made me more alert for signs that anything out of the ordinary was taking place.

Several months after my last visit from the creatures, I was working late in my office one evening while my sons were watching a movie in the living room. By this time, my boys were all in their teens. The next day they relayed an experience that didn't make sense to me.

My youngest son, who was 15 at that time, told me that his two older brothers had seen an owl outside the living room window.

"Why didn't you guys come get me?" I asked him. An owl at our window would certainly qualify as an unusual thing and something I imagined would have created excitement. We hadn't seen an owl outside of an animal park before so to have one outside our window would have surely been exciting enough to warrant them barging into my office for me to come see it. They've barged in for lesser things.

"I don't know," he answered.

"Did you see it?" I asked him.

"No," he told me. He told me his oldest brother saw the owl at the window and mentioned it.

Apparently my oldest son had mentioned it in a casual way saying, "hey, there's an owl at the window." At that point, my second son had gone and looked at it. Strangely, my youngest son did not go look at it.

I found this whole story hard to believe since having an owl outside the window would be so unusual that someone would have come and gotten me to go see it as well. At the very least, they would have come and told me as soon as it had left.

I asked my oldest son about it and he said they were watching a movie and he heard something at the window so he got up to go look out and there was this big owl, about two feet tall, sitting on the ledge outside the window staring in. He couldn't tell me the color of the owl, only that it had big round black eyes.

He then called his brothers to the window and only Nick went to see it, and he too was just staring at it. Apparently, they both just stared at it until eventually it went away. Neither of them knows how long they stared at it and neither of them felt excited enough about it to come tell me. My youngest son at the time couldn't explain why he didn't go look at it as well, but when asking him about it today he says he doesn't even think he was in the room and his memory of it is foggy. He only remembers that his two older brothers saw an owl on the window ledge.

Once my two oldest sons described their experience of staring at this owl perched outside the window, I went to the window the owl was apparently at. I pointed out to the boys that not only have I never heard of an owl being two feet tall, although that didn't mean that there weren't two feet tall owls, but also there *was* no ledge outside the living room windows (or any of our windows) that an owl, or even a small bird, could perch on. The outsides of our windows are flush with the building. They couldn't deny this but they were both just baffled and confused over how this 'owl' had managed to perch outside the window for an extended period of time with nothing to actually perch on.

Several months later, in May of 2007, my oldest son moved out and into his own apartment and my middle son, Nick decided to move to Alberta to live with his father. My youngest son went with us on the drive to the Halifax airport and later that day as we were driving home I saw an object in the sky.

It was still daylight out and out of nowhere, quite far off in the sky ahead, was what appeared to be a spherical silver shiny ball in the sky.

"Look, there's a UFO," I said to my son, pointing at the sky.

"Where?" he asked, looking towards where I was pointing.

I never took my eyes off it and as soon as he asked where I watched it disappear before my eyes. It went from being a solid spherical silver object to being absolutely nothing. It didn't fly away; it faded away. I watched it as it faded to invisible.

I told him that it had just disappeared and I don't think he believed me. I think he thought I was playing a joke on him or something but I wasn't.

It was within next week that I had my only experience that I'm aware of involving missing time. I am sure of the time frame because my son left for Alberta on May 20th and I quit my job with the news on May 31st.

I worked from a home office, monitoring news stations for a huge news clipping company called Cision Canada. My job involved recording news broadcasts, writing up summaries of them and entering it into the company's database. Most of the news broadcasts I monitored were recorded elsewhere and I simply downloaded the media files to monitor, but one local two-hour talk show was recorded on tape at my office. The two-hour show ran from 9am until 11am and was recorded on a tape that held one hour on each side.

My morning routine had been the same for the full 13 years that I'd worked for the news. I left the radio that recorded the talk show turned up so that when it came on at 9 A.M to record the show, it would wake me up. I would get up, check my watch, turn down the radio, walk through the office, turn on my computer, go to the bathroom, walk down the hall to the kitchen and turn on the dishwasher, go back to my office and begin work at 9:15. My routine was very important because the news was so time sensitive and I had to get my morning news in by 10 A.M. At 10 A.M., I would get dressed, eat breakfast and be back at my desk at 11 A.M. to start the talk show that had just finished recording.

So, on this particular morning my routine started out as it had every other morning. At 9 A.M., my talk show radio went off full blast. I checked my watch and it said 9 A.M. I got up, turned down the volume on the radio, walked through the office and turned on my computer, then went on to the bathroom. I then went down the hall to the kitchen and started the dishwasher and went back to my office to start my morning news.

I sat down at my computer and saw that the time on my computer said 11:30 A.M. I thought, *that's weird, somehow the time got screwed up on my computer, I hope I don't have a computer virus.* So, I opened the time change function and looked at my watch to get the exact minute to set the clock to.

I was shocked when my watch *also* showed that it was 11:30 A.M.

This is impossible, I thought. A few minutes ago it was only 9 A.M., it should be 9:15 just the same as on every other morning when I sat down at my desk. I was totally confused as to how both my computer *and* my watch had suddenly malfunctioned and both displayed the exact same incorrect time.

I was so confused so I left my office and went out in the kitchen to check the kitchen clock. To my surprise, that clock also said it was 11:30!

This is impossible, I kept thinking over and over. I had woken up, looked at my watch and it was 9 A.M., I had walked through the office, to the bathroom and the kitchen and nothing had taken me any longer that morning than any other morning. I had walked back to the office and it should have been 9:15. No matter how many times I went through the steps in my mind, nothing added up. This just did not make sense.

Okay, I thought, desperately seeking logic. *If it is really 11:30 then that would mean that only the first hour of the talk show recorded because I know I didn't turn over the tape at 10 A.M. If it is really 11:30 then only one side of the tape will be recorded and not turned over and the radio would have shut itself off at 11:00.*

I ran into the office and pulled out the tape. It was still on Side 1 and had not been turned over. It was definitely after 11:00 because the machine shuts itself off at the end of the two-hour program at 11:00 and it was off.

Oh my God, I thought. This meant I had missed my morning news deadline. I knew I'd be getting an email from my boss demanding to know why I'd missed my morning deadline. I was in a panic as I realized that not only did I have no excuse for my boss, I didn't even have a clue what had happened myself! I *know* I had gotten out of bed at 9 A.M.; I had looked at my watch as I was getting up.

I rushed through my morning news then wrote up the one hour of the talk show that had recorded. I was completely baffled as to what kind of explanation to give my boss. I settled on the absolute truth and sent off an email that said simply, "for some reason, only the first hour of the talk show got recorded." It was truly for *some* unfathomable reason.

Once I was finished my morning news, it was already time to do my lunchtime news, so I scrambled to do that. Then, immediately after that was a two-hour afternoon talk show to do, followed by the suppertime news, a one and a half hour public affairs show, and then a brief break before a four-hour evening show. During my brief break, I had supper with my son and then did some research on missing time.

I originally started out checking to see if this could possibly be a symptom of a brain tumor or epilepsy or something. I did this despite the fact that several times in my adult life I had tests done that determined I do not have any form of epilepsy. I had heard of missing time phenomena in relation to alien abductions before but there was no way that *this* could be *that!* I had not seen a UFO, beings, or anything odd that morning. I had not had one split second where anything seemed out of the ordinary. There was not one second where I could possibly pinpoint the disruption in time had occurred.

I looked at my watch when I'd gotten up; it was 9 A.M.. I walked to my office, turned on the computer, walked down the hall to the bathroom, used the bathroom and washed up, walked to the kitchen, started the dishwasher and walked back to the office and sat down. There was not an available moment where it could have, or should have, suddenly *become* two and a half hours later!

It wasn't like I was driving along some road in the dark and found myself parked on side the road and then drove home and ended up home two and a half hours later than I should have been. This was broad daylight! I never left my apartment! At what point, if I'd been abducted, would it have happened? While I was standing by the dishwasher? While I was in the actual process of walking down the hallway? Surely not while I was sitting on the toilet! Thinking back on it now, the only moment that isn't clear in my brain is around the time period I was washing my hands and face in the bathroom. That memory is a bit fuzzy.

Concerned that I may have had some sort of brain malfunction, I searched the Internet for symptoms of brain tumors, epilepsy, Alzheimer's, and any other brain issue I could think of. None of the symptoms included what I'd experienced that morning. So then I added the term 'missing time' to my search query and I got a list of symptoms relating to UFO abduction.

The list was a check off list of symptoms and experiences to determine if a person was a possible abductee. The list sent shivers up my spine as I realized I'd experienced an alarming number of things on that list, including:

Seen lights in the sky

Seen objects in the sky

Seen beings in my bedroom

Experienced missing time

Had feelings of being away and returning

A fear of being outside alone

A fear of the dark

An interest or fear of UFO's and aliens

A terminated pregnancy with no fetus.

Psychic abilities

Inexplicable feelings of aversion to heights, snakes, spiders, large insects, certain sounds, bright lights, personal safety and/or a fear of being alone.

You have had times when you found blood, or small drops of blood on your pillow with no explanation how it got there.

You have had nose bleeds at some time in your life without apparent cause or you have awoken with a nose bleed. (For only a brief period of time when my kids were little I would have sudden short nosebleeds for absolutely no reason.)

Have you ever been or are you now afraid of your closet or any closet in the house, having to make certain the door(s) are always shut?

You have the feeling you should not talk about these things or that you are not supposed to talk about these things

You have experienced many of these traits but cannot remember anything related to any abduction experience.

These were just a few items on this long list of signs that had taken place in my own life.

My mind went reeling over my past. I had had four miscarriages in my life. I had a miscarriage in my first month of pregnancy when I was 21. This was followed by a successful pregnancy for my oldest son. After his birth, I had quickly gotten pregnant again when he was only three months old. When my son was 8 months old, I had a miscarriage. I was five months pregnant and had felt the baby kick. After being rushed into the delivery room and the ordeal was all over, I asked to talk to the doctor.

"I would just like to know if the baby was a girl," I asked. Since I had successfully given birth to a boy and this was my second miscarriage I had a fear that I might only be able to carry boys and not girls. Whether that is even possible, I don't know, but I asked.

"I don't know," he answered.

"What do you mean you don't know?" I asked in surprise. He was a doctor and had just delivered a five-month-old fetus and couldn't tell if it was a girl or boy yet? "Well, what did it look like?"

"I…don't know," he said again with a puzzled look on his face.

"What do you mean?" I asked again. Why wasn't he telling me? Had the baby been deformed or something and he just wasn't telling me? "You couldn't tell if it was a boy or girl? Was it deformed?"

"I …don't know," he said again, looking bewildered. "There was no baby. It didn't develop, I guess. There was nothing there."

"What do you mean, nothing there?" I demanded, getting a bit hysterical. "I felt the baby kick! I felt it move! I've had five prenatal checkups and everything has been fine up until now! What do you mean, there was nothing there?"

This was a complete mystery to me, and apparently my doctor as well. He seemed completely baffled. Way back then, though, I had not read anything about missing pregnancies or alien abductions or anything.

Six months later, I got pregnant for my middle son, then got pregnant for a fourth time but had another miscarriage. With that one, again there was no fetus but I was only three months pregnant and in the midst of dealing with my husband cheating on me, so I was not in an emotional state to really question the presence of a fetus. Again, that was before I'd done any reading on this phenomena in relation to UFO's and it was back before the Internet.

Nine months later I had my fourth miscarriage. This one was only one month along. A year later, I got pregnant for my third son. He weighed 9 lbs and has had unusually high intelligence. He was able to read and discuss grade 9 science books when he was 7 years old in grade 2. He, as a teenager, has experienced seeing orbs fly around him.

CHAPTER SIX

It has taken me a long time to write this book. It took me a long time to even share my experiences with anyone. When I first started telling people about the creatures I've seen, I would become terrified at even speaking about it. I felt that just speaking about them would call them back. I drew a picture of the creature and once I'd showed my son the picture, I erased it. I had drawn it in pencil because I felt that even having drawn the picture would bring the creature back. When I decided to draw what I'd seen, I knew that I could only do this if I did it in pencil so I could erase it immediately afterwards. As soon as my son looked at it, I snatched the picture back and began erasing it and then shredded the piece of paper. My fear was so strong and I was so afraid of doing anything inadvertently to draw them back to me.

When I first met my current partner, a year after my last visit from these creatures, I felt safe in telling him everything that had happened to me. At that time, I didn't piece everything weird in my life together as relating to each other, but I shared the two obvious related incidents of the two visits from these small hooded creatures. At that time, I hadn't remembered that the small creature I'd seen in the back porch when I was three years old was one of these same creatures.

I felt safe in telling my experiences to my new partner. To my shock, he not only believed me but said he had also seen small hooded creatures when he was a kid and his sisters and brothers saw them too! I felt further trust and relief when he shared his experience of seeing a UFO land in a wheat field across the road from his farm when he was a teenager. He and his two younger brothers had seen it. It was huge with lights all around it.

Once I realized that I truly wasn't alone in seeing strange things, it became easier to open up and tell others. I began telling my sisters of my strange experiences. They still didn't believe me, but it no longer mattered to me who believed me and who didn't. I realized how good it felt to talk to someone who believed me and had seen strange things as well, and decided that someday perhaps my sharing my experiences would help others to not feel the same sense of aloneness that I'd felt before I found my current partner.

I started telling everyone anytime the subject of paranormal events, aliens or UFO's came up. To my surprise, many people have seen lights in the sky.

In March of 2009, I woke up one day in March with the strong urge to go to Ecuador. I told this to my partner and his only response was, "Okay, let's go!"

I did some research and found that an old friend of mine was living in Vilcabamba, the Valley of Longevity in the Andes Mountains of Ecuador. I decided that was where I needed to go, to this little village high in the Andes. It was only after I decided that that I discovered that this was a hotspot for UFO sightings. Many people, including my old friend that lives there, told me that they'd seen strange lights in the sky. Some locals told me that there is a legend that the aliens hid gold in Mandango Mountain and that they come back for it. Mandango is also known as the 'sleeping lady' that protects the village since its profile appears to be a lady sleeping.

Many UFO's are apparently seen over that mountain, although I have never seen any during the six months that I spent in Vilcabamba. I must admit, however, that I didn't actively watch the sky for them while I was there. Although, there were two nights that I saw a very bright light above the house that was bright enough to shine through the bedroom drapes. I hadn't dared to get up the first night and in the morning, when I told my partner, he just said it must have been the moon. I checked the Internet and found out that it was not a full moon at that time, in fact, it was a new moon and there was no moon in the sky at all! Four nights later, the bright light came back shining in the window. This time, since I'd been ridiculed the first time for not doing so, I got up and peeked out the window from the edge of the drape. The light was directly above the house so I couldn't really see much more than the very edge of a big white light above us. It was too far up in the sky to be a street lamp and bright enough to be the moon, but I didn't think it was the moon.

Since I was not brave enough to go outside to get a good look at it, and couldn't really see it well enough from the bedroom, I will write that one off as possibly being the moon. I only mention it here because at that time, it was certainly not the time for a full moon and why it suddenly appeared over the house, I don't know. As I said, I could go either way on that one, but the fact that I'm so fearful of things in the night now is obviously evidence of post-traumatic stress.

The two nighttime traumatic experiences that I remember have left me with phobias. At 45, I still don't dare to stay alone in a house at night. I still have an aversion to being outside alone in the daytime even. I have near panic attacks if I am in an open field by myself.

The field thing may have deeper meaning since I used to play in our field as a kid. During my childhood I became afraid of being out in the field alone and would only go across the driveway to play in the field if my siblings went with me. On at least one occasion when I experienced the feeling that I'd just returned from somewhere, I found myself standing near the edge of the field.

Again, I have no firm conclusions about what has been happening to me, other than I'm experiencing strangeness. Do I think aliens abducted me? No, I don't. I don't ever recall seeing the inside of a spaceship. The beings I've seen don't bear any resemblance at all to what others have described as aliens. I do not think the beings I've seen came from another planet.

Up until this point I've experienced extreme anxiety when sketching the beings I've seen in order to show someone. Usually the sketches are immediately destroyed as soon as the person that wants to see them have done so. However, spending six months in the Andes Mountains has somehow made me braver.

I don't know whether it is because I met so many people there that had seen strange lights in the sky and the legends of UFO's and aliens are well known to the locals, or whether it is because this is the time, but I no longer feel like it is 'not right' for me to write about this. Over the years, several times I've tried to start writing a book about these experiences, but every time I got the distinct feeling that it was the wrong thing to do and I would scrap the idea and destroy the first few paragraphs I'd written.

But after my quest to find others that have seen what I've seen and experienced exactly what I've experienced, I've realized that it wasn't answers that I was looking for but just the confirmation that someone believed me and could relate. So, I am writing this not to give answers, but to put this information out there so that the next time that someone does a search for 'small brown hooded creatures' they will find images they're looking for and know they're not alone.

IMAGES

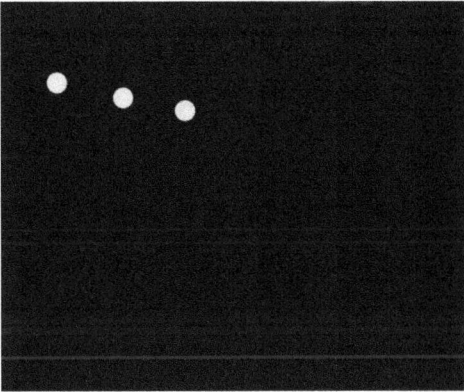

The three lights we saw in the sky on our way to Yarmouth.

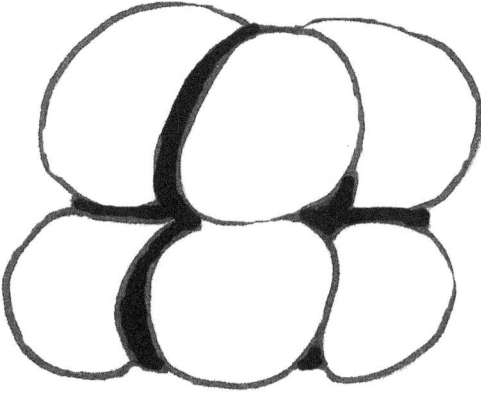

The image stuck in my head after my 'away' experiences as a child.

The small hooded creatures dressed in monk-like hooded robes. They had so many wrinkles, appearing very ancient.

A Friendly Giant imposter accompanied my first encounter with the hooded creature when I was 3 years old.

My second encounter with the hooded creatures involved one sitting on me and touching my forehead with a silver wand.

My third encounter with the hooded creatures involved them apparently healing my kidneys in the middle of the night, 10 years after my second encounter with them.

My dream in which a strange medical scanner created a 3D holographic image of my organs on a glass table in the middle of the room.

www.ingramcontent.com/pod-product-compliance
Lightning Source LLC
Chambersburg PA
CBHW032034090426
42741CB00006B/803